**Lea**
(1

.oan p

fine
rt of
:rdue

FAMOUS PEOPLE
FAMOUS LIVES

Biographies of famous people to
support the curriculum.

# Marie
# Curie

by Karen Wallace
Illustrations by Nick Ward

**W**
FRANKLIN WATTS
NEW YORK•LONDON•SYDNEY

First published in 1998 by
Franklin Watts
96 Leonard Street
London
EC2A 4RH

Franklin Watts Australia
14 Mars Road
Lane Cove
NSW 2066

ISBN: 0 7496 2942 8

A CIP catalogue record for this book
is available from the British Library.

Dewey Decimal Classification Number:  JB / CUR

10 9 8 7 6 5 4 3 2 1

Series editor: Sarah Ridley
Series designer: Kirstie Billingham
Consultant: Dr Anne Millard

Printed in Great Britain

# Marie Curie

Marie Curie was born in Poland
in 1867. Her Polish name was
Marya Sklodowska and she had
three sisters and a brother.
Marie's father taught science and
her mother ran a small school.

Marie grew up in a happy family. Her father could speak six languages and told them stories from many countries.

One day Marie was looking at her father's cabinet filled with mysterious test tubes and bottles. She asked him a question that would change her life.

Marie's happy life was soon hit by tragedy. When she was eight, her sister Sofia died of typhus. Two years later her mother died of tuberculosis. Marie was very depressed and the whole family went through a very sad time.

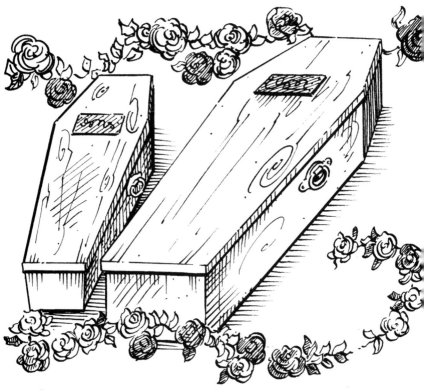

Marie and her sister Bronya were very clever at school. They both wanted to continue their studies. At that time in Poland, only boys could go to university.

At first the future seemed hopeless for Marie and Bronya.

Then Marie had a brilliant idea. They would both work to send Bronya to Paris in France to study medicine. When Bronya became a doctor she would send for Marie and support her.

The plan worked! In 1890
Marie climbed on a train to
Paris. To save money, she
travelled in an open carriage
and took all her belongings
with her.

Paris astonished Marie. It was so different from Poland. People were free to read what they wanted. They were free to study what they chose.

Marie began her studies at university where there were twelve thousand other students.

13

Soon Marie decided to move nearer to the university. She did not want to waste precious hours travelling back and forth from Bronya's apartment.

All she could afford was a tiny garret room but at least she could study during all her spare time.

In July 1893, when she was twenty-six, Marie took her degree in Physics. She had only been in Paris for eighteen months and she was very nervous. The result came as a complete surprise.

Marie immediately decided to study for a second degree, in Maths. That next year, two very important events happened in her life. She gained her Maths degree and she met her future husband.

Marie, let me introduce you to Pierre Curie. He is a great physicist.

19

Marie and Pierre were married a year later. They shared a love of science and worked brilliantly together.

On the rare occasions they took time off, they went on cycling tours around France.

In 1897 Marie's first daughter, Irene, was born. Marie also published her first scientific work, on steel and magnetism.

Her next big project was an advanced degree called a doctorate. There was only one problem.

One particular discovery caught her eye. A German physicist called Dr Röntgen had discovered some strange rays.

The rays were able to pass right through the body and show all the bones inside. Dr Röntgen didn't know what name to give them so he called them x-rays. As proof of his discovery, he used the x-rays to take a picture of his wife's hand.

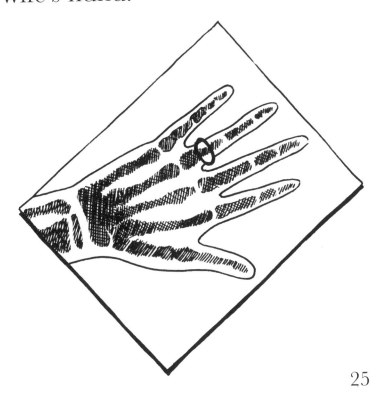

Soon afterwards a French scientist called Henri Becquerel discovered that these rays were produced by an element called uranium.

He called the rays 'uranic' rays but did not investigate further. Marie made a decision.

Marie's first job was to find out if any other elements contained the mysterious rays. At that time, scientists knew of eighty-three different elements.

29

Marie found out that one other element, called thorium, also gave off these same rays. She called them radioactive rays.

Then she tested a tar-like mineral called pitchblende. She discovered it gave off rays eight times stronger than uranium, yet contained no thorium.

There was only one answer. There must be a new element no-one had yet discovered!

Marie and Pierre worked with
tons of pitchblende. It was hard,
dirty work. The pitchblende
had to be boiled, filtered,

And yet this is all we have.

PITCHBL

dissolved and turned into crystals. At each stage elements were removed to leave the tiniest amount of pure radium.

By 1902 Marie had finally prepared a tenth of a gram of pure radium. The following year, her research was rewarded by a special degree called a doctorate in Science.

Your achievement is remarkable.

Soon scientists all over the world were making extraordinary discoveries. Radium and radioactivity led scientists to understand how atoms work and provided the first hope of a cure for cancer. But the greatest glory for the Curies was still to come.

*Daily News*

MARIE AND PIERRE CURIE SHARE NOBEL PRIZE FOR DISCOVERY OF RADIUM WITH HENRI BECQUEREL

NOVEMBER 1904

Today a huge honour was bestowed on Pierre and Marie Curie.

The following December
Marie's second daughter, Eve,
was born.

Shortly afterwards, Pierre was
made a Professor of Science at
the Sorbonne University.

Then in 1906, tragedy struck. Pierre was run over by a wagon and died instantly. Marie was shattered but buried her grief in work.

We have made you a Professor at the Sorbonne. Will you take over your husband's work?

Yes. It is what Pierre would have wanted.

When Marie was forty-four, she was awarded her second Nobel Prize for her work measuring the purity and strength of radium. This work was vital to the new treatment of cancer.

The following year building
began on the Radium Institute
in Paris. Marie planned the
garden herself.

Three years later, in 1914, the
First World War broke out. With
the help of her elder daughter
and other volunteers, Marie set
up a fleet of x-ray ambulance
units. This helped doctors to
find and remove bullets from
wounded soldiers.

When the war ended, there were two hundred x-ray units in military hospitals. The only problem was Marie's own health.

After the war, there was a
desperate shortage of radium.
The United States agreed to
provide more if Marie went on
a fund-raising lecture tour.

At first Marie was reluctant. She was not well and she was naturally shy. Eventually she agreed and the visit was a great success.

Over the following years,
Marie continued her work but
her health got worse.

Although she didn't know it, she had radiation sickness caused by years of handling radioactive material. Scientists today wear protective clothing.

Marie Curie died at the age of sixty-six in 1934. She was undoubtedly the greatest woman scientist of her time.

# Further facts

## New Discoveries

Since Marie Curie's
lifetime, scientists
have discovered many
more elements.
There are now over a
hundred. Ninety-four
occur naturally on Earth.
The others have been created in
the laboratory.

## Kill or Cure

We now know that radiation can
*cause* cancer as well as *cure* it. It can
also weaken the body's defence to
disease. Nowadays researchers take
many precautions to shield themselves

from any kind of
contact with radiation.
They wear protective
clothing and limit
the time they spend

working with radioactive material.

## A Family Affair

Marie's elder daughter
Irene also became a
famous scientist. She and
her husband, Frederic
Joliot, won the Nobel Prize in 1935 for
their work producing radioactivity
artificially. Sadly, Irene also died
prematurely of radiation sickness.

# Some important dates in Marie Curie's lifetime

**1867**  Marya Sklodowska, later Marie Curie, born in Warsaw.

**1885**  Bronya goes to Paris. Marya works as a governess.

**1891**  Marya begins her studies at the Sorbonne.

**1893**  Marie comes first in her Physics degree.

**1894**  Marie takes her Maths degree and meets Pierre Curie.

**1895**  Marie marries Pierre.

**1897**  Irene, their daughter, is born on September 12.

**1902**  Marie and Pierre produce the first radium.

**1903**  Marie is awarded her doctorate. The Curies win the Nobel Prize with Henri Becquerel.

**1904**  Eve is born.

**1906**  Pierre is killed in a road accident.

**1911**  Marie wins her second Nobel Prize.

**1914**  War breaks out. Marie starts mobile x-ray units.

**1921**  Marie visits America to raise money for more radium.

**1934**  Marie dies of radiation sickness.